CONTENTS

BRING A TORCH, JEANETTE ISABELLA

CELLO

17th Century French Provencal Carol
Arranged by CHIP DAVIS

GOOD KING WENCESLAS

CELLO

Arranged by CHIP DAVIS

CAROL OF THE BELLS

Ukrainian Christmas Carol
Arranged by CHIP DAVIS

CELLO

CHRISTMAS LULLABY

CELLO

By CHIP DAVIS

DECK THE HALLS

CELLO

Arranged by CHIP DAVIS

GOD REST YE MERRY GENTLEMEN

CELLO

19th Century English Carol
Arranged by CHIP DAVIS

13

GREENSLEEVES

CELLO

Sixteenth Century Traditional English
Arranged by CHIP DAVIS

HARK! THE HERALD ANGELS SING

CELLO

By FELIX MENDELSSOHN
Arranged by CHIP DAVIS

JOY TO THE WORLD

CELLO

Arranged by CHIP DAVIS

PAT A PAN

Words and Music by BERNARD DE LA MONNOYE
Arranged by CHIP DAVIS

CELLO

SILENT NIGHT

CELLO

Arranged by CHIP DAVIS

TRADITIONS OF CHRISTMAS

By CHIP DAVIS

CELLO